REMARKABLE LGBTQ LIVES™

Zachary QUINTO

AN ACTOR REACHING FOR THE STARS

MONIQUE VESCIA

ROSEN
PUBLISHING®

New York

REMARKABLE LGBTQ LIVES™

Zachary QUINTO

AN ACTOR REACHING FOR THE STARS

Published in 2015 by The Rosen Publishing Group, Inc.
29 East 21st Street, New York, NY 10010

First Edition

Library of Congress Cataloging-in-Publication Data

Vescia, Monique.
Zachary Quinto: an actor reaching for the stars/ Monique Vescia.—First edition.
    pages cm.—(Remarkable LGBTQ lives)
Includes bibliographical references and index.
ISBN 978-1-4777-7893-7 (library bound)
1. Quinto, Zachary—Juvenile literature. 2. Actors—United States—Biography—Juvenile literature. I. Title.
PN2287.Q56V47 2015
791.4302'8092—dc23
[B]
                                        2014007272

Manufactured in China

CONTENTS

INTRO

Zachary Quinto might have the most distinctive pair of eyebrows in show business. Black, bushy, and highly expressive, those trademark brows have been used to great effect in Quinto's portrayal of deeply disturbing television villains such as Sylar in *Heroes* and Dr. Oliver Thredson on season two of *American Horror Story*. Though he excels at playing bad guys, the thirty-six-year-old Pittsburgh native has managed to avoid the pitfalls of typecasting, something he proved when he won the role of Mr. Spock in J. J. Abrams's *Star Trek* films. Having played one of the most iconic characters in the universe in a series of blockbuster movies, Quinto might have been tempted to believe he'd fulfilled all his career goals. Nonetheless, he used that big-screen success as a springboard and returned to his roots in live theater. He earned raves as Louis Ironson in *Angels in America* and made his Broadway debut as Tom Wingfield in Tennessee Williams's classic play *The Glass Menagerie*.

DUCTION

Zach, as his friends call him, became interested in theater from an early age. It offered him a safe refuge and a place to dream. With plenty of hard work and persistence, Quinto has become a well-respected actor with a multitude of credits in television and film. He also helped form a media production company, which has released acclaimed films such as *Margin Call, All Is Lost*, and *Banshee*

A talented actor as well as a successful film producer, Zachary Quinto has also made headlines as an outspoken supporter of gay rights.

Chapter. Quinto's success in so many ventures seems to prove one of his core beliefs, "that the universe will support you if you're specific about what you want."

This highly talented and versatile actor, praised by critics and fellow cast members alike, is also an eloquent spokesman for the causes in which he believes. A longtime supporter of gay rights, Quinto always knew that his coming out as a gay man would be in his own time, on his own terms. His decision to finally speak frankly about his sexual orientation was triggered by a tragic event: the suicide of Jamey Rodemeyer, an openly gay teenager, who took his own life after being relentlessly bullied by his classmates.

Gay, lesbian, bisexual, and transgender teens are five times more likely to commit suicide than their heterosexual peers, according to one Columbia University study. Quinto, who was bullied in high school for being gay, has turned his despair at these losses into positive energy and action. He channeled it into political activism on behalf of gay rights. The actor and producer donates his time and star power to anti-gay-bullying campaigns and the fight for marriage equality.

Celebrities have a lot of influence in contemporary culture, and Quinto has consistently used his fame to send a message of tolerance and love. In interviews, at science fiction and comic book conventions, and on Twitter, Reddit, and Instagram, he stays upbeat, and reminds his fans to stay focused on what is truly important: finding a way to bring people together in mutual respect. Quinto is very specific about what he wants, as quoted in a *New York Times* article: "I would love to be a voice in this maelstrom of chaos and obsessive celebrity infatuation that says, 'Let's talk about something that matters.'"

CHAPTER 1

STEEL CITY CHILDHOOD

On June 2, 1977, in Pittsburgh, Pennsylvania, Joseph "Joe" and Margaret "Margo" Quinto welcomed their second son, Zachary, into the world. Another son, named Joe, had been born six years earlier. The boys' Italian-Irish heritage came from their father's Italian background and their mother's Irish ancestors. In Pennsylvania and other U.S. cities, members of these immigrant groups often intermarry, since many among these two populations share a Catholic faith.

Zachary and his family lived in Green Tree, a borough of Pittsburgh. Joe Quinto Sr., a Pennsylvania native and U.S. Navy veteran, worked as a barber. The Quintos regularly attended church services, and Zachary sang in the church choir and served as an altar boy. When they weren't in school, the brothers enjoyed running around in the woods and riding their bikes.

Pittsburgh is strategically located at the juncture of three rivers, where the Allegheny and the

Once home to both the Pittsburgh Pirates baseball team and the Steelers football team, Three Rivers Stadium was imploded in 2001, when the Steel City's sports teams moved to newly built arenas.

Monongahela meet to form the mighty Ohio River. First known as the Iron City and then as the Steel City, Pittsburgh flourished as the United States demanded steel for the construction of buildings, bridges, ships, and railroads.

World War II created more jobs for workers in steel mills and factories. During the war, the Pittsburgh region produced more steel than Japan and Germany combined. However, by 1977—the year Zachary was born—Pittsburgh had become a city in crisis. The once-powerful steel industry had collapsed as a result of foreign competition and its failure to modernize. Today, Pittsburgh's population has shrunk to less than half of what it was in 1950.

Despite its economic woes, the city still benefited from many important cultural institutions established during boom times. Sometimes called "the Paris of Appalachia," Pittsburgh boasted institutions such as the Carnegie Museums and the Pittsburgh Symphony and Opera. Zachary's parents made sure that he and his brother attended plays and shows. Zachary loved going to the theater and was especially struck by a production of the musical *Sweeney Todd.* As it would turn out, being exposed to live theater from an early age helped Zachary to discover his life's purpose.

A PIECE OF GAY RIGHTS HISTORY IN PITTSBURGH

In 1972, the Pittsburgh television program *Hotline* aired a call-in show featuring gay activist Randolfe (Randy) Wicker. Wicker was the first gay man to openly appear on television (on *The Les Crane Show* in 1965). The show was intended as an educational tool, to help inform callers (as well as the host of the show) about gay life and dispel myths and rumors about homosexuality. You can view this remarkable TV artifact today online.

A TERRIBLE LOSS

In 1984, when Zachary was only seven, his family suffered a devastating loss: his father died, rather suddenly, of kidney cancer. Losing him was a terrible blow to Zachary, his mother, and his older brother, who was taken on fishing and camping trips by Joe. Judging from the community's response to Joe Quinto's death, he must have been a remarkable man, described by his youngest son as "really badass and confident and intelligent and sensitive and curious." Zachary has said, "For years after he died, people would go out of their way to let me know how much he meant to them."

After the boys lost their dad, Joe Jr. became the father figure in his little brother's life. He kept a close eye on Zachary and disciplined him when he felt it was necessary. Margo Quinto had to take on clerical work to support the family, which meant she was now away from home when the boys returned from school. Hard as the experience must have been for a young boy, Zachary has said that losing his father ultimately helped make him more independent and self-reliant. He also believes that the loss of his dad helped develop his imagination. "I don't know that I would have been so self-sufficient and so ambitious if I hadn't lost him," Quinto has said. "It triggered some sort of survival instinct in me."

Even though he now divides his time between Los Angeles and New York, Quinto is still a proud son of his hometown of Pittsburgh, Pennsylvania.

After his father's death, Zachary's interest began to shift from the church to theater. He became a talented mimic, and his teachers recognized early signs of his acting and musical abilities. The theater was a place he could go where his mother knew he was safe while she was away at work.

EARLY INFLUENCES

Zachary was about nine years old when he began to realize that he was gay. At the time, he tended to brush these thoughts aside, since he didn't know what to do about it.

Positive role models, in the arts and in life, can help young people discover and shape their own identities. But for a kid growing up in Pittsburgh, Pennsylvania, in the 1980s, who had begun to understand that his sexuality didn't conform to the heterosexual norm, gay role models were largely nonexistent. Gay characters were almost entirely absent from the mainstream movies and TV shows of the time. As Quinto told *Rolling Stone* critic Peter Travers in an interview, "I never had anyone to look [up to] in that position."

He was bullied in high school for being gay, though he did not officially come out until years later. Still, Quinto was not an angry kid, and he developed skills that would come in handy later in life: "I can

Quinto as Mr. Spock, Chris Pine as Captain Kirk, and Zoe Saldana as Lieutenant Uhura share a tense moment in the film *Star Trek into Darkness*. Young Zach probably never dreamed he would one day wear the ears of one of TV's most iconic characters.

always talk my way out of a fight. It taught me a lot about psychology."

When Quinto went to the theater to see a play or a musical, he could escape—for a while, at least—the pressures of growing up without a father, of being menaced by other kids at school, of feeling like he didn't fit in. He could lose himself in the marvelous spectacle that was taking place before him on the stage. And he could begin to imagine what it might be like to be standing up there himself.

IN THE WINGS

When Quinto was growing up in Pittsburgh, reruns of *Star Trek* were broadcast on TV. The program attracted a wide and devoted audience in syndication and became a cult classic, airing in 94 percent of the United States by 1994. Quinto, however, was not a fan. He preferred watching *Duck Tales* and *20/20,* a current affairs program.

Star Trek fans appreciated how the show managed to push boundaries and explore ideas that wouldn't have been acceptable in a more realistic setting. Series producer Gene Roddenberry used the science fiction setting of the show to address many of the social issues of the 1960s, when the program was originally made. Subjects such as sexism, racism, and nationalism were examined in various episodes. The series featured the first depiction of an interracial kiss between Captain Kirk, a white man, and Lieutenant Uhura, an African American woman. At the time, that kiss was considered groundbreaking, and it was deeply

Contemporary social problems were often addressed within the science-fiction setting of *Star Trek*, where beings from different alien races often coexisted peacefully.

disturbing to some viewers with more traditional values.

Television is a far more personal medium than the big screen. People view television shows in the privacy of their own homes. This helps explain why black characters, gay characters, and members of other minority groups were regularly featured on TV screens years before they appeared in mainstream

Actress Amanda Donohoe, who played the attorney C. J. Lamb, made television history in February 1991 when her character locked lips with another woman in an episode of *L.A. Law.*

films. Still, it wasn't until 1991 that a same-sex couple was shown kissing on television. In the popular NBC series *L.A. Law*, actress Amanda Donohoe played a bisexual lawyer, who kissed a female colleague on the lips. Certain viewers protested the show, and advertisers threatened to pull their ads in the resulting controversy.

Like most kids, young Zachary didn't spend his time worrying about who was on television and who wasn't during those years when he was growing up in Pittsburgh. He was far more interested in picturing himself onstage, acting and singing in big musical productions just like the performers he went to see at the theater.

"THE PARIS OF APPALACHIA"

Quinto's birthplace, Pittsburgh, has always celebrated and supported the arts. Though the nickname has ironic overtones, since Appalachia is often associated with extreme rural poverty, the city boasts a designated Cultural District, a fourteen-block area in the heart of downtown that includes Heinz Hall, Benedum Center for the Performing Arts, the Pittsburgh Opera, the Pittsburgh Ballet Theatre, the August Wilson Center for African American Culture, and other cultural landmarks.

A MINI STAR IS BORN

Early on, people recognized that young Zachary Quinto had theatrical talent. In class he was outgoing and social, and he had a good singing voice. When he was in fourth grade, Quinto's music teacher, Miss Smith, sent him home with a note about trying out for the CLO Mini Stars, a performance group for young actors that is part of the Pittsburgh Civic Light Opera (CLO) organization. Founded in 1946, CLO has been bringing musical theater to the city of Pittsburgh and launching the careers of talented performers for decades.

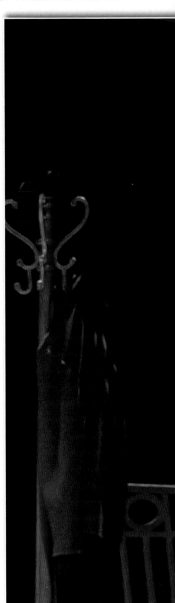

Quinto was excited by the idea and decided that he wanted to audition for Mini Stars. Eventually, he earned a spot in a show, and at age eleven he made his musical theater debut as a Munchkin in a CLO production of *The Wizard of Oz*. He was ambitious, even then; in a recent interview with *Backstage* magazine, Quinto said he was devastated not to be cast as the mayor of the Munchkins. The production was held in the 2,800-seat Benedum Center, at the center of Pittsburgh's Cultural District.

Quinto loved being onstage, and he continued acting in plays and musicals, including *Much Ado About Nothing*, *Cinderella*, and *Oliver!* Jill

Quinto's early love of live theater would eventually help him to achieve every stage actor's dream: a starring role on Broadway.

23

Wadsworth, Quinto's first acting instructor, remembers him as more mature than the other students. He also devoted a lot of his free time to worthy causes. While he was in high school, Quinto volunteered with the Boys Club of Western Pennsylvania. He also served on the Youth Advisory Council, helping organize community service activities in support of the homeless, youth at risk, and the elderly. As a member of the Youth Volunteer Corps, Quinto worked to involve other teens in various volunteer efforts.

Quinto's first real job was at a hardware store in Green Tree. He recalls, "It was kind of boring, but I liked mixing paint and making copies of keys for customers." He earned his first acting award during this

THE GENE KELLY AWARDS

The Pittsburgh Civic Light Opera's National High School Musical Theater Awards, also known as the Jimmys (in honor of legendary Broadway theater owner and producer James M. Nederlander), recognize individual artistry in vocal, dance, and acting performance by high school students from around the country. Winners of the regional Gene Kelly Awards, named after Pittsburgh native Gene Kelly, dancer, actor, singer, director, producer, and choreographer, compete in the Jimmys. The Gene Kelly Award annual honors are given in the categories of Best Actor, Best Actress, and Best Supporting Actor and Actress. Zachary Quinto shares this honor with Broadway veteran Michael McGurk, Courtney Mazza, Chris Peluso, Christian Elan Ortiz, and others.

time: the 1994 Gene Kelly Award as Best Supporting Actor (see sidebar), for his role as Major General Stanley in Central Catholic High School's production of *The Pirates of Penzance*. However, he didn't really get serious about a career as a professional actor until a fateful moment forced him to see his future in a different light.

BLACK ICE AND A FATEFUL DECISION

On a cold night in December, when Quinto was sixteen and a junior in high school, he and three friends went for a drive. Quinto was behind the wheel of his mom's car, and it was the first time she had allowed him to take it out. The boys were joking and laughing and probably driving a little too fast along Serpentine Drive in Schenley Park, next to the Carnegie Mellon University campus. Quinto didn't see the patch of black ice, and when the wheels hit this slick spot, he lost control of the car and slid off the road.

Luckily, none of the boys was hurt, but one of the car's axles was broken in the accident and the vehicle had to be towed away. Quinto's mother was furious, and later that night, the two had a long and heated exchange. Margo Quinto saw the accident as a metaphor for her younger son's life; he seemed to have spun out of control on the road of life, and she wanted to know what he planned to do about it.

This argument with his mother, painful though it was, turned out to be a watershed event in Quinto's life—the moment when he realized that he wanted to become a professional actor. Arriving at this decision gave Quinto a focus for his life; from then on, the choices he made were governed by his ambition to establish an acting career. And Pittsburgh was a good place for an aspiring young actor to start out because it has so many excellent resources to draw upon. Gazing out the window of his advanced placement English class, with its view of the adjacent Carnegie Mellon University campus, Zachary Quinto plotted his next move.

DRAMA SCHOOL DAYS

F ounded in 1914, the Carnegie Mellon School of Drama is the oldest degree-granting drama program in the United States. By enrolling there, Quinto could get a world-class theatrical education and still have Sunday dinner with his mom. An audition is required as part of the application process.

The School of Drama at Carnegie Mellon University prepares its graduates for the many challenges of a career in theater, film, or television.

Quinto, former Munchkin, was now 6'4" (1.93 m) tall, with dark brown hair, brown eyes, and boldly expressive eyebrows. He was handsome in an interesting way, and highly intelligent, and he moved well and gracefully. He aced his audition and earned a place in the program, entering in the fall semester of 1995.

All students in this conservatory training course take the same core curriculum of classes in acting, voice, speech, and movement. At Carnegie Mellon University, Quinto arranged to room with his friend Rob Boldin, a vocal performance major. The two had met at a high school choral festival and stayed in touch. The work in the drama program was intense, and the roommates rarely saw each other during the long days, but they caught up whenever they could.

Part of the preparation involved certain theatrical exercises; one with which all the freshman drama students became familiar was called Before the Door. A door is set up in the classroom, surrounded by an assortment of props. The exercise requires the actor to imagine that on the other side of the door is an obstacle or an intense situation that he or she does not want to face. The actor must improvise a scene that occurs before the door is opened. Other skills that a stage actor must master include how to project his or her voice, use body language to convey character, stage a fight, and cry on cue. Before the Door and other drama exercises helped Quinto hone his craft as an actor.

UNCLOSETED HOLLYWOOD

Since the beginning of the movie industry, many famous actors and actresses have hidden the truth about their sexual orientation from the public for fear of damaging their careers. Sometimes the decision to pose as a heterosexual was an actor's personal choice; sometimes it was because of pressure by the studios, which released staged publicity shots of stars dating members of the opposite sex. Sometimes stars entered "New York marriages" (or marriages of convenience) to squelch rumors about their sexual orientation.

In the increasingly progressive climate of the twenty-first century, however, many actors (as well as professional athletes and newscasters) have chosen to come out of the closet or were never closeted to begin with. In recent years, Wentworth Miller, Raven-Symoné, Maria Bello, Maulik Pancholy (*30 Rock*), Sara Gilbert (*Roseanne*), and Jodie Foster all made public statements about their sexual orientation.

FROM COLLEGE FRIENDS TO BUSINESS PARTNERS

At CMU, Quinto met many people who would become important in his life and influence his career. One of these was Neal Dodson, who enrolled at CMU a year after Quinto. The two young men had met at a summer acting program in 1994, where they had performed Shakespeare's *Romeo and Juliet*, with Quinto playing the part of Mercutio to Dodson's Romeo.

They became friendly with Corey Moosa, another student in the drama program. After graduation,

Power trio: (*from left to right*) CMU alums Neal Dodson, Zachary Quinto, and Corey Moosa attend the New York premiere of *All Is Lost*.

Moosa moved to New York, where he established himself in the downtown theater community. The friendship between Quinto, Dodson, and Moosa would eventually grow into a thriving business partnership. Reflecting on his experiences in the program, Quinto says, "I think of my time at Carnegie Mellon as the most creative and most expansive time I've ever experienced. . . .It was a four-year playground."

SHOWCASING TALENT

In the final year of spring semester, seniors graduating from Carnegie Mellon School of Drama have the opportunity to show off their talents at two Senior Showcases of New Talent, one held in New York and the other in Los Angeles. At these showcases, aspiring

Pittsburgh, shown here, was in close enough proximity to Manhattan that Quinto could set his sights on the New York stage and its world-class theater scene.

seniors can network with casting directors, producers, agents, and other important people working in film, theater, and television in the United States and around the world. The showcases afford CMU graduates an excellent opportunity to launch their careers.

Because of Pittsburgh's proximity to New York and the vibrant theater scene there, Quinto focused most of his hopes on his New York Showcase. Los Angeles has long been considered the center of the American film and television industries, and New York's Broadway is the epicenter of live theater in the United States. Quinto, whose BFA degree is in musical theater, was surprised when he drew more favorable responses from his Los Angeles showcase. After discussing his options with friends, he decided that a move to California might help jump-start his career as a professional actor.

Quinto's experience at CMU was overwhelmingly positive and helped him make some very influential friendships. However, in an interview with radio host Howard Stern, Quinto admitted that if he were just beginning his career, he probably would not enroll in drama school. He believes that acting has to be a natural gift; an actor with natural talent can refine his craft in school, but he cannot acquire talent in a drama program if he doesn't already possess it. The industry has changed, and Quinto feels that, as a result, the value of such an education has diminished. The rise of so-called reality TV

FAMOUS ALUMS OF CMU DRAMA SCHOOL

Zachary Quinto is in excellent company as an alumnus of the CMU Drama School. Currently ranked number four in the world by the *Hollywood Reporter*, the CMU program has launched the careers of actors such Ted Danson, Holly Hunter, Blair Underwood, and the award-winning writer/producer/director Steven Bochco (*Hill Street Blues*; *L.A. Law*; *Doogie Howser, M.D.*).

means that people become celebrities not because they are talented and well educated but because they are willing to sacrifice their privacy and integrity to be famous.

Nonetheless, the value of a formal education is not limited to the knowledge and skills that one acquires; it also includes the people one meets and the mentors and professional relationships one cultivates. Quinto's network of CMU connections would prove to be very useful down the line.

A NEW VENUE IN THE NEW MILLENNIUM

Relocating to Los Angeles in 2000 after graduating from Carnegie Mellon was a bit of a culture shock for Quinto, who had always imagined himself in New York doing live theater. It helped that his older brother, Joe, already lived in L.A., where he was working as a professional photographer. Joe, who has photographed many actors and musicians, helped his brother by creating a series of headshots of Zachary. Head shots are formal portraits that actors use to promote themselves to agents and casting directors, and they can make or break an acting career. Like many a struggling actor before him, Zachary was waiting tables to pay his rent, in one case working the notoriously slow "graveyard shift" (11:00 PM to 7:00 AM) between auditions.

Wearing black tie and a fashionable "five o'clock shadow" of razor stubble, Zachary Quinto arrives on the red carpet.

BREAKING INTO THE BUSINESS

Quinto's first on-camera job came six weeks after his move to Southern California. He appeared in a commercial for Surge, a citrus soft drink, since discontinued. He filmed several other commercials, as well as a few guest spots on television.

After three months in Los Angeles, Quinto landed his first pilot, *American Soap*, opposite Jonathan Taylor Thomas, who also appeared in the sitcom *Home Improvement.* Unfortunately, as often happens in the TV business, the show was not picked up, and Quinto began waiting tables again. Around this time he also starred in another unsold pilot, *An American Town* (2001).

One day his agent called with exciting news: Quinto had been cast in a recurring role ("Tony") on an NBC supernatural mystery series called *The Others.* The cast also included *Star Trek: Enterprise* actors John Billingsley and Bill Cobbs, as well as another Carnegie Mellon alumnus, Gabriel Macht. Much to Quinto's disappointment, however, the show was soon canceled.

Work was sometimes slow to come, but eventually Quinto managed to rack up a series of guest appearance on TV shows such as *Touched by an Angel* (2001), *CSI: Crime Scene Investigation* (2002), *The Agency* (2002), *Charmed* (2003), *Six Feet Under* (2003), *Joan of Arcadia* (where he appeared as God)

His trademark eyebrows hidden behind a pair of shades, the dog-loving actor steps out for a stroll in Los Angeles with a furry friend named Noah.

(2005), and *Crossing Jordan* (2006), among others. He also managed to score some work in film: He had a small, uncredited role in a thriller called *Psychic Murders* (2002), and in the romantic comedy *Down with Love* (2003) he played an angry beatnik. For a talented, ambitious, and impatient guy like Quinto, real success still seemed very elusive.

Suddenly, Quinto's luck improved: He was cast as tech agent Adam Kaufman in the popular Fox series *24*, starring Kiefer Sutherland as counter terrorist unit agent Jack Bauer. The acclaimed drama was gearing up for its third season, had already won two Emmy Awards, and had been nominated for Golden Globe Awards and Screen Actors Guild Awards.

Eventually, *24* would surpass *Mission Impossible* and *The Avengers* to become the longest-running spy-themed television drama. Quinto's character was

THE GLAAD MEDIA AWARDS

The Gay & Lesbian Alliance Against Defamation awarded its first GLAAD Awards in 1990 to honor the 1989 season. The award recognizes various branches of the media for their fair, inclusive, and accurate representations of the lesbian, gay, bisexual, and transgender community. In 2013, *American Horror Story: Asylum*, in which Quinto appeared, won GLAAD Media Awards for two episodes.

originally supposed to be featured only a few times, but as it turned out, he appeared in twenty-three of the program's twenty-four episodes. Working with the cast of a weekly television drama was an extremely useful experience for Quinto. But after season three, with no explanation, his character was written out of the show.

DARK DAYS AND DISAPPOINTMENTS

Then Quinto was cast in a faux-reality series on VH1 called *So NoTORIous*, loosely based on the life of actor

Tori Spelling, daughter of the famous TV producer Aaron Spelling. Quinto plays Sasan, a gay Iranian-American who is one of Tori Spelling's close friends. Openly gay to his friends, Sasan must hide his sexual orientation from his parents. The program debuted in 2006 and was

Friends onscreen and off, Zachary Quinto and actress Tori Spelling have some fun at the VH1 screening party for *So NoTORIous*, held at Jimmy's Lounge in Hollywood.

QUINTO'S SHORT FILMS

Boutonniere is a ten-minute film by first-time director Coley Sohn, a friend of Quinto who asked him to appear in his movie. *Boutonniere* is about a teenage girl who wants to graduate high school and move away from her overbearing mother, but first she must survive her mom's plans for the senior prom that she doesn't want to attend.

Quinto played a character named Michael Paul David, a shopkeeper who helps the girl and her mother find a prom dress. "He just let me put him in braces and horrible pants and shoes, and he was just a great sport," Sohn said in an interview. In 2009, *Boutonniere* was a Sundance Film Festival selection.

Another short film, called *Dog Eat Dog*, was nearly two years in the making. Quinto and Sian Heder raised money for the project with the crowdfunding site Kickstarter. The campaign brought in more than $30,000—four times their original fund-raising goal, some of which was donated to the U.S. Humane Society. *Dog Eat Dog* presents a funny and true but exaggerated account of Quinto's adoption of his rescue dog, Noah, from an animal shelter. The thirteen-minute short debuted on Petsami, the YouTube channel for animal lovers.

canceled after only ten episodes, despite earning critical acclaim. In 2007, *So NoTORIous* was nominated for a GLAAD Media Award.

Quinto's contract with *So NoTORIous* prevented him from auditioning for any other acting roles. By the time the show was canceled, he had missed his chance to audition for shows in the upcoming season. Finding himself unemployed again with no prospects, Quinto became depressed.

Six months passed with no acting work. He remembers this as one of the darkest periods of his life. He stopped shaving, grew a scraggly beard, and was filled with uncertainty and frustration about his stalled career. It had been nearly seven years since Quinto had graduated from drama school, and now he was a twenty-eight-year-old, out-of-work actor who couldn't seem to catch a break. Little did Quinto know that all the darkness he was carrying around inside would serve him well.

CHAPTER 5

RECURRING ROLES

S hortly before his thirtieth birthday, several things happened in quick succession that changed Zachary Quinto's life. First, he received a callback after an audition he'd done for a new TV series called *Heroes*. The science fiction drama, which aired on NBC from September 2006 to February 2010, tells the story of a group of individuals from around the world who discover that they each possess certain superpowers. *Heroes*' main characters include a cheerleader who cannot be injured or killed, an artist who paints scenes of the future, a beautiful Las Vegas showgirl with a dangerous alter ego, a politician who can fly, a cop who reads people's minds, a prison inmate who can walk through walls, and a Japanese comic-book geek who can make time stand still. Eventually, the characters find they all share a common destiny: they must band together to save the world.

Quinto began his work on the show as a guest star in "Seven Minutes to Midnight," an episode in

Flanked by fellow cast members (*left to right*) Hayden Panettierre, Leonard Roberts, Adrian Pasdar, and Rena Sofer, a grinning Quinto celebrates the wrap of the first season of *Heroes*.

season one of *Heroes*. Twenty-four episodes later (of which he appeared in fifteen), he was promoted to a series regular with the airing of "Kindred." At first, viewers of the show saw only a shadowy, menacing figure known as Sylar; his face was hidden by a baseball cap and he appeared in silhouette. On "Seven Minutes to Midnight," the mysterious Sylar was revealed to be Zachary Quinto when he stepped into the light to threaten Hayden Panettiere, who played cheerleader Claire Bennet. Before Quinto's appearance in the eighth episode, various stunt doubles played the role of Sylar.

As the show progressed, viewers learned that Sylar was actually the pseudonym for Gabriel Gray, the son of a watchmaker who had continued in his father's profession. Gray lives with his mother, who constantly tells her son that he is special and deserves more from life. It turns out she's right: her son is special. Sylar, who takes his alias from a brand of watch, turns out to have a supernatural ability of his own: when he murders someone, usually by cutting open the skull of his victim, he assumes that person's superpower.

SYLAR'S DARK APPEAL

Unlike his recurring role as the computer genius Adam Kaufman on *24*, Quinto's part on *Heroes* was central to that drama. Audiences were captivated by the serial killer with superpowers, whose personality turned out to be far more multifaceted than the average supervillain's. Quinto's skill as an actor allowed him to bring out surprising aspects of the character and to endow Sylar with a complex inner life. Quinto's talents helped give the character additional depth and substance: "We both have a desire to be valued. My desire to be valued is manifested in

Quinto brought depth and complexity to the supervillain Sylar and won the NBC series many new fans.

cultivating relationships with my friends and family. Sylar's desire to be valued manifests itself...well, in a murderous rampage." His unnerving stillness lends Sylar a particular kind of menace. As Quinto said in a 2007 interview, "There's a lot of power in stillness. I learned that in my years at school and it's something that really serves this character."

During the third part of the drama ("Villains"), the show's writers turned Sylar into a hero temporarily and had him team him up with Claire's adoptive father, a character initially referred to as "Horn-Rimmed Glasses," or "HRG." Unfortunately, after its compelling first season—thanks largely to Quinto's Sylar—the show failed to live up to its initial

ACTORS ON ZACH: COSTARS TALK ABOUT QUINTO'S CRAFT

"Sylar's the coolest thing because he's so unpredictable and so downright evil. It's almost hard for me to watch because it's the polar opposite of Zach's personality; he's just the kindest, gentlest, most giving person." —*Heroes* co-star Kristen Bell

"As an actor you always want to work with someone who'll elevate your work. He's so talented...I just look up to him so much." —*Heroes* co-star Dania Ramirez

promise. The plots became increasingly confusing, and the characters did not develop. In May 2010, *Heroes* was finally cancelled.

BUILDING A FAN BASE

Heroes appealed to many comic book fans. Quinto soon attracted a large and devoted fan following, and he began making appearances at conventions. The actor has said of his fan interactions, "One thing that people always say to me is, you're the nicest villain I've ever met." *Heroes* fans remain ever-hopeful that the series will be resurrected. One fan group calls itself Sylar's Army, or the "Sarmy." Their slogan is "Every villain needs a legion of evil supporters," and they do charity work on the character's behalf. The Sarmy raises money for causes that Quinto supports, such as the Epilepsy Foundation. They also sell T-shirts, teddy bears, and coffee mugs featuring images of the character that *TV Guide* called one of the "Sixty Nastiest Villains of All Time."

Instead of scaring people off, Quinto's dark good looks inspired a lot of online swooning from people of both genders. (He was named one of *People* magazine's "Sexiest Men Alive" in 2007.) There was also plenty of heated speculation about his sexual orientation. Rumors paired him up with his *Heroes* costars Hayden Panettiere and Dania

Quinto and Jonathan Groff enjoy the sunshine on a shopping trip to a Los Angeles farmers' market.

Ramirez, as well as Rumer Willis (daughter of Bruce Willis and Demi Moore), and *Glee* TV star Jonathan Groff. (Groff was the only one of these people whom Quinto actually dated.) Even though Quinto came out to his family when he was twenty-four, and his close friends knew he was gay, he had avoided going on record about it when he spoke to the press. His rationale was that it was, after all, nobody's business. As Quinto told the audience at a Fan Expo appearance, "The line between my public self and my private self is very clear."

Being cast as the main antagonist in *Heroes* marked a turning point in Quinto's career. The success that followed was a direct result of how well he had portrayed such a dark character. "My point of entry for a lot of characters tends to be their shadow," he says. "I'm a big believer in the notion that our greatest potential lies in our darkest parts. To a certain extent, it's only in facing those parts of ourselves that we can truly grow, and I think that's true of all of the characters I've played, certainly in the past few years."

HORROR SHOW

Quinto's skill at portraying disturbing characters later won him recurring roles on the TV series *American Horror Story*, starring veteran actress and two-time Oscar winner Jessica Lange. The series, which has attracted a cult following, features a self-contained

In his major small-screen roles, Quinto has treated viewers to some truly disturbing characters, such as *American Horror Story*'s sociopathic Dr. Oliver Thredson.

storyline for each season. In season one (*Murder House*), Quinto played Chad Warwick, one half of a gay couple that lived in the cursed house around which the story is centered. In the second season (*Asylum*), Quinto returned to the show as the sociopathic psychiatrist Dr. Oliver Thredson, whom he has called "the most despicable character I've played."

Asylum takes place during the 1950s in a mental institution for the criminally insane, and Dr. Thredson is a court-appointed psychiatrist with psychological issues regarding his relationship with his mother. Various episodes explore the themes of demonic possession, abuses in the mental health system, racism, and homophobia. The series' edgy social

FAN FICTION FAVORITE

Popular TV, film, and literary characters have inspired a phenomenon known as fan fiction (or fanfic). Fans develop new plots and construct fictional stories featuring their favorite characters and settings. Though the practice has gained popularity with the evolution of the Internet, fan fiction has existed for centuries, since printed books became widely available. Zachary Quinto's gallery of fascinating characters has inspired reams of fictionalized tales written by his fans, which can be read online. You can try your hand at writing your own fan fiction. Be aware, however, that publishing it online might well violate existing copyright laws.

content helped earn *American Horror Story* seventeen Primetime Emmy nominations in 2013, making it the most nominated show that year. Quinto was nominated for Outstanding Supporting Actor in a Miniseries, but his costar James Cromwell took home the Emmy for his role as Dr. Arthur Arden.

In the recurring roles of Sylar and Dr. Thredson, Quinto successfully wormed his way into the consciousness (and nightmares) of television audiences. Fans who loved his work in *Heroes* couldn't wait to see what this talented actor could do on the big screen. They were about to find out.

CHAPTER 6

TO BOLDLY GO: THE
STAR TREK MOVIES

I n the midst of the excitement he had gener-
ated as the villain Sylar in *Heroes*, Quinto never
stopped thinking about what his next step would
be. During this time, he received an e-mail from a
friend who mentioned the new *Star Trek* movie, based
on the original TV series, that J. J. Abrams would
be directing. The film was in pre-production, and
Abrams planned to assemble an all-new cast to play
the iconic roles of the crew members of the starship
Enterprise: Captain James T. Kirk, Mr. Spock,
Dr. McCoy, Mr. Sulu, and Lt. Uhura, among others.
The e-mail included a link to a website where fans
had created a list of actors they wanted to see play
the pointy-eared half-human, half-Vulcan Mr. Spock.
Quinto's name was on the list.

Quinto wasn't a big science fiction fan when he
was a kid. Though he had seen episodes of the TV
show when he was growing up, he would never have
labeled himself a *Star Trek* fan, or Trekkie, unlike his

Leonard Nimoy, who originated the role of Mr. Spock on the original *Star Trek* TV series, wrote an autobiography titled *I Am Not Spock.*

college friend Corey Moosa. But suddenly something clicked in his head. Later that night at a party, he found himself telling a friend, "They're making a new *Star Trek* movie. I'm going to play Spock."

his journal so that he could pr

When he returned for his

It didn't hurt tha

Greg Grunberg

mind-read

Hero

..ad

p   .ud serious

ac......iiops." Word started
getting around.

Six months later, Quinto
finally got his chance to
audition for the part of
Spock. There was a lot of
secrecy surrounding the
film, and the actors who
auditioned for different roles
were not allowed to take
the script home to study it.
Quinto went to the casting
office and asked to read the
script to help prepare for his audition. He was left
alone with a copy for forty-five minutes. He took the
opportunity to scribble down some of the dialogue in

...ctice it later at home.
...audition, Quinto was ready.
...t J. J. Abrams's good friend
...who played Matt Parkman, the
...ng policeman on
...s, couldn't stop rav-
...ng about costar Quinto's
talents on the set.

ACING THE AUDITION

Quinto first auditioned for the part of Mr. Spock on the morning of April 15, 2007. He wore a blue shirt and flattened his hair down when he met with *Star Trek* casting directors April Webster and Alyssa Weisberg. Coincidentally, it was the day after the original Spock, Leonard Nimoy, had presented Quinto and his *Heroes* castmates with a Future Classic Award at the TV Land Awards. Despite such a positive omen,

director J. J. Abrams was not initially convinced that
Quinto was right for the part. He scheduled a meeting
with him on June 5, and this time Quinto succeeded
in winning Abrams over. Two days later he was offered

Matching tuxedos and
trophies: The male cast
members of *Heroes* take
the stage at the Fifth
Annual TV Land Awards.

the role of Spock. It was Quinto's first major feature film, and he would be playing one of the most iconic characters of all time.

The official announcement that Zachary Quinto had been cast as Mr. Spock in the *Star Trek* remake was posted the following month on the E! Online July 23 edition, but rumors had been swirling for weeks. Fans who had backed Quinto as their top choice for Spock were over the moon. He was the first actor cast in the film, months before his costar Chris Pine secured the role of Captain Kirk. One reason Pine was offered the part was that he and Quinto belonged to the same gym and became friends. In the film, Leonard Nimoy would be playing the older Mr. Spock (called Spock Prime) in an alternate time line.

Quinto was still appearing in the second season of *Heroes* when he was cast in *Star Trek*, which created a potential conflict. However, the Writers Guild of America, the union that represents many film, TV, and radio writers working in the United States, had threatened to go on strike. Compared to writers' salaries in the big film studios, television writers were not well paid; when their demands weren't met, the union initiated a writers' strike that lasted for more than three months, from November 5, 2007 to February 12, 2008. During that hiatus, the movie *Star Trek: The Future Begins* was filmed.

PASSING THE VULCAN MANTLE

Leonard Nimoy and Zachary Quinto met for the first time in an elevator at ComicCon International in San Diego on July 26, 2007. As Quinto describes it, they hadn't yet been formally introduced, and they rode in awkward silence as the elevator inched its way toward their destination. As the elevator doors slid open, Nimoy turned to Quinto and told him, "You have no idea what you're in for," before walking away.

Quinto and his costar and friend Chris Pine, as Captain Kirk, teamed up to launch *Star Trek* into the next millennium.

Despite this rather chilly beginning, the relationship soon warmed up. On the set of the film, Nimoy gave Quinto pointers about the character he had so memorably originated. Quinto adopted Nimoy's habit of standing with his hands clasped behind his back. He initially had trouble making the Vulcan salute with his right hand, and he bound his fingers together with rubber bands to practice that gesture. As the two Spocks spent time together, they realized they had a lot in common besides the iconic character each had had the good fortune to play. Eventually, the two became close friends and filmed a car commercial together that spoofed their relationship (see sidebar on page 66).

SPOCK ON SPOCK

In 2008, at a Star Trek convention in Las Vegas, Nevada, Leonard Nimoy answered questions about what it was like to see Zachary Quinto in the role of Spock: "It was very moving to me. You know, I'm seventy-seven years old and it's time for me to move on...A lot of people say he looks just like me, but he's a very, very good actor, very intelligent. He's well-trained. He knows his business, his work, he's very professional. And if it had been a lesser actor it could have been disturbing for me to see the character pass on to somebody who I didn't think was appropriate...I'm very pleased that the character passed on to him. I think it's in good hands."

A TALE OF TWO EYEBROWS

The part of Mr. Spock is a challenging role for an actor. Most of the time, the character must remain very restrained and unemotional, befitting his highly rational Vulcan nature. As played by Leonard Nimoy, Spock's most expressive gesture was a quizzically raised eyebrow. Furthermore, since Spock is actually half human, elements of his personality are in conflict with each other, the emotional human side at odds with the rational Vulcan side. In a May 2013 interview with the Reuters news agency, Quinto said that Spock's nature is "the head versus the heart. That is certainly something I can relate to. As someone who has been considered pretty intellectual and wordy, I also have a deep well of emotional life. I understand what it means to be in constant relationship with both those aspects of myself."

As Quinto once remarked, with tongue in cheek, when asked about the similarities between himself and Mr. Spock, "My eyebrows are a huge part of my life, and his eyebrows are a huge part of Spock's life." He also joked about the fact that when he was a kid, he had sported a bowl haircut similar to Spock's. For Quinto, whose bushy eyebrows dominate his face, the physical transformation into the character proved to be time-consuming and painful. Quinto had to show up on set around 3:00 AM, several hours before his fellow cast members. His eyebrows had to be shaved and plucked and new brows applied. The makeup artists also had to give him Spock's characteristic pointed Vulcan ears. Sometimes Quinto slept through the process or used the time to study the script and prepare for his upcoming scenes. When the movie was filmed, Quinto's older brother, Joe, even got into the act: he performed stunts as a Romulan Narada crew member.

THE VULCAN SEAL OF APPROVAL

Leonard Nimoy made it quite clear that he was happy to have Zachary Quinto follow in his Vulcan footsteps. He praised his co-star publically in interviews and at fan conventions: "I saw Zachary Quinto do things with the character that had never occurred to me, which I found quite delicious. I think he really

has found a way to expand the character while at the same time…being true to the character." Many members of the vast and vocal fan base of *Star Trek*, known as Trekkies, also embraced Quinto's younger

Live long and prosper: Quinto flashes the famous Vulcan salute, a gesture that Leonard Nimoy (*left*) introduced when he was cast as the original Mr. Spock.

version of Spock. Overall, the *Star Trek* remake garnered very positive reviews, earning a 95 percent
approval rating on Rotten Tomatoes, an aggregate
website that summarizes movie reviews.

Quinto signed a contract to play Spock in at least
two sequels of the film, and the first of these, *Star
Trek into Darkness*, was released in May 2013. The
sequel proved disappointing for some audiences,
especially hardcore Trekkies. At a Star Trek convention in Las Vegas, fans of the TV series awarded *Star
Trek into Darkness* the dubious title of the worst *Trek*
movie ever made. Perhaps most controversial was a
scene in which Quinto's Spock screams out the name
of "Khaaaaannnn!!!" in a very un-Vulcanlike burst of
anger. But Trekkies are a notoriously tough crowd; the

SPOCK VS. SPOCK

The car company Audi aired a hilarious ad called "The Challenge"
featuring the old and the new Mr. Spock. Timed to coincide with the
release of *Star Trek into Darkness*, the two-minute-plus commercial
features Leonard Nimoy and Zachary Quinto. After losing to Nimoy
in a game of 3-D chess played on iPads, Quinto challenges him to a
game of golf; the last person to reach the club pays for lunch. Nimoy
sets out in his Mercedes, singing to himself about Bilbo Baggins (a
character in *The Lord of the Rings* and *The Hobbit*). When Quinto
beats him, driving the Audi S7, sneaky Nimoy drops him with a
Vulcan nerve pinch and wins the race. The commercial ends with
both Spocks remarking "Fascinating," as the driverless Audi
heads off to park itself.

general public showed far more enthusiasm for the film, and it pulled in more than $450 million worldwide at the box office.

The third *Star Trek* movie, which Abrams will not direct, is yet to be filmed at the time of this writing. Quinto will be spending plenty of time in that makeup chair, and he isn't complaining. To his surprise, he discovered that his background in live theater had unexpectedly prepared him well for the role of Spock: "I never would have imagined science fiction to factor so prominently in my career, but I'm glad that it has. I think science fiction tends to be very theatrical. I come from a theatrical background. There's something about the canon of *Star Trek* which is almost evocative of a Shakespearean dynamic in terms of the epic storytelling, characters that come in and out of sweeping narratives, and stakes that are really high."

TAKING A STAND

Appearing in the new *Star Trek* franchise as
Mr. Spock helped make Zachary Quinto a
household name. To date, he is the only
person who has appeared on the cover of consecutive issues of *Entertainment Weekly* magazine, first as
Sylar in the cast of *Heroes* (issue #1018, on October
31, 2008) and then as Spock (#1019, November 7,
2008). Suddenly he was a celebrity, but the majority
of his audience did not know that he was gay.

There was a great deal of speculation about his sexuality, however, especially on the Internet. Quinto had
always been outspoken in his support of gay rights and
marriage equality, and he had volunteered his time to
the Trevor Project (http://www.thetrevorproject.org).
Founded in 1998, the nonprofit is the leading national
organization for crisis intervention and suicide prevention for gay, lesbian, bisexual, transgender, and
questioning teens and young adults. He also had supported other gay rights activities, such as the *Laramie*

A somber-looking Quinto attends the opening-night party for the revival of *Angels in America*. The epic play has also been produced as an opera and a TV miniseries.

69

Project, a play that calls attention to the absence of hate crime laws in many states. Quinto had publically opposed the U.S. military's "Don't Ask, Don't Tell" policy toward gay service personnel, which was repealed in 2011. However, he deflected interviewers' questions about his sexuality and insisted on keeping that part of his life private.

In 2010, Quinto heard that playwright Tony Kushner and director Michael Greif were planning an off-Broadway revival of the epic *Angels in America: A Gay Fantasia on National Themes*, Kushner's Pulitzer Prize–winning play about the HIV/AIDS epidemic. First performed on Broadway in 1993, the monumental two-part play was Kushner's response to the loss of an entire generation of gay men to the ravages of HIV/AIDS.

At that time, before the disease became more fully understood and before medications were developed to relieve its symptoms, an AIDS diagnosis was a death sentence. Early in the history of the disease, many people didn't understand that it could not be spread by casual contact, such as hugging or tears or sweat. Infected individuals were often regarded with fear and stigmatized. Some considered AIDS a punishment for homosexual behavior, and blamed the victims of the so-called "gay plague."

Quinto auditioned twice for the play and landed the role of Louis Ironson, one of the leads and perhaps the play's most challenging role. Ironson, who is gay, abandons his lover when he is stricken with AIDS. After performing on a hit TV series and in a blockbuster film, Quinto was deeply gratified to be onstage again, as he said: "I moved to L.A. ten years ago so that eventually I'd be able to come back to New York to do a play." He'd started his work as an actor on the stage, and it was a place he'd always planned to return.

Angels in America opened on October 28, 2010, and Quinto earned glowing reviews for his portrayal of the self-involved Ironson, a complex character who is tortured by guilt. The playwright intended the evolution of Ironson's character to mirror the audience's own, moving from fear and selfishness to an ultimate acceptance of moral responsibility.

ON HIS OWN TERMS

Nearly a year later, in October 2011, Quinto sat down at a café in Manhattan's East Village to give an interview with Benjamin Wallace, a reporter from *New York* magazine. He began by reflecting on the success of his eight-month run in *Angels in America*, and told Wallace that the play was "the most challenging thing I've ever done and the most rewarding." It made him feel lucky he was born when he was, too young to be among that generation of men lost to AIDS. Then Quinto went on to say something he had never said before to a member of the press: "[A]s a gay man, it made me feel like there's still so much work to be done." Later in the interview, he repeated the phrase, "as a gay man," just to make sure his message was received loud and clear.

This was the first time Quinto had publicly acknowledged his sexual orientation. His decision to do so was prompted, he later explained, by the despair he felt when he read about the suicide of fourteen-year-old Jamey Rodemeyer of Buffalo, New York. Rodemeyer was an openly gay teenager, who had spoken out against homophobia on the It Gets Better video project. He was bullied for years at school and online about his sexuality.

Even though Rodemeyer had promised, in his video, that it is possible to triumph over such negative experiences, it proved too much for him. He eventually chose to take his own life. During

the run of *Angels in America*, Quinto had made his own video for the It Gets Better campaign. He had also been bullied in high school, and the problem of antigay bullying was something he cared about

Family and friends of fourteen-year-old Jamey Rodemeyer, a victim of antigay bullying, gather at a candlelight vigil held in his honor in Williamsville, New York.

deeply. Now the time had come for the world to know exactly where he stood in relation to this issue: "I believe in the power of intention to change the landscape of our society, and it is my intention to live an authentic life of compassion and integrity and action. Jamey Rodemeyer's life changed mine."

Later, when he was questioned about why he chose to come out when he did, Quinto explained that he'd always known that this revelation would be "in my own time, on my own terms." He didn't discuss the decision with his agent in advance. He'd reached a point in his life where he believed that "absolutely no good could come from. . . being quiet" about his sexuality.

Besides Rodemeyer, a number of other gay teens had recently committed suicide as a result of homophobic bullying. In the face of these tragedies, Quinto felt he owed it to Rodemeyer and other gay teens to declare himself a gay man, and to stand in solidarity with them against such vicious homophobic attacks. As he later said in an interview with the *Huffington Post*, "I thought about it as coming out from behind the wall. Walls now are only as high or as thick or as strong as we allow them to be."

MIXED REACTIONS

Quinto was between *Star Trek* films when he made his announcement. He had not told J. J. Abrams, director of the films, that he was going to come out of the closet. The news spread at warp speed online and via social media websites like Twitter and Instagram. Given the homophobia and gay bashing still present in American culture, some fans undoubtedly were disturbed by Quinto's revelation. Below online articles in which the actor speaks candidly, some of the posted comments contain antigay remarks and hateful responses. However, what impressed Quinto was how supportive people have been, by and large, about his decision to openly declare himself a gay man.

THE QUINTO EFFECT

Word of Quinto's coming out proved inspirational to many people. One of them was Mitch Anderson, a high school senior in Belton, Texas. An All-State swimmer and class salutatorian, Anderson had never before found the courage to tell anyone he is gay. He decided to come out during his graduation speech, delivered on June 7, 2013, when he announced to the assembled crowd:

"I feel the moment has arrived for me to be publically true to my personal identity. So now, I can say, I'm gay. It is both a significant portion of who I am and an inconsequential aspect. It's as natural and effortless to me as breathing."

Mitch went on to talk about standing up to homophobia and not allowing it to diminish your own self-worth: "I believe Zachary Quinto put it best by saying, 'If people don't want to work with me because of my sexual orientation, then I have no interest in working with them to begin with.'"

Quinto believes that coming out has not hindered his acting career one bit. Hopefully, he is correct. Even ten years ago, it would have been hard to imagine an openly gay actor starring in a blockbuster action movie franchise like *Star Trek*, but attitudes are definitely changing. One recent poll showed that 58 percent of voters nationwide support the freedom to marry, including 81 percent of voters under the age of thirty.

GAY RIGHTS ACTIVISM

Well-known actors and other celebrities frequently lend their muscle to political causes in which they believe. Quinto, who publically backed gay causes even before coming out, has championed many important organizations and projects that support LGBTQ rights. One of these, in 2009, was a one-night benefit presentation of *Standing on Ceremony: The Gay Marriage Plays*. TV celebrities Debra Messing of *Will and Grace* and Jason Alexander of *Seinfeld*, among others, donated their time and star power, and Quinto participated in a staged reading of twelve new plays inspired by the debate over gay marriage surrounding California's Proposition 8.

The so-called California Marriage Protection Act, an attempt to ban same-sex marriages in that state, was struck down by the Supreme Court in 2013. As

THE LARAMIE PROJECT

In October 1998, Matthew Shephard, a twenty-one-year-old gay student at the University of Wyoming, was robbed, tortured, tied to a fence, and left to die outside Laramie, Wyoming. Shephard's murder brought worldwide attention to the terrible consequences of hate crimes. Public outrage eventually spurred legislation known as the Hate Crimes Prevention Act, which was signed into law by President Barack Obama in 2009.

The Laramie Project is a play by Moisés Kaufman and members of the Tectonic Theater Project that was inspired by Matthew Shephard's murder. The three-act play incorporates material from hundreds of interviews conducted with the residents of Laramie, news reports, and the actors' own journal entries. *The Laramie Project* has been performed in high schools, colleges, and community theaters around the United States, and in playhouses around the world, as part of an effort to combat homophobia and raise consciousness about hate crimes.

Ten years after the murder, members of the Tectonic Theater Project returned to Laramie to conduct follow-up interviews with residents whose words were featured in the play. *The Laramie Project: Ten Years Later* premiered as a reading at 150 theaters in the United States and internationally on October 12, 2009, the eleventh anniversary of Shephard's death.

Quinto once said, he considers the movement for marriage equality "an unstoppable wave." Many people agree that the fight for equal rights for all people, regardless of sexual orientation, is the new civil rights movement of the early twenty-first century, as the fights for women's rights and racial equality were in the twentieth century.

At a TrevorLIVE event honoring singer Katy Perry and Audi of America, Quinto hams it up with some affirmative speech bubbles.

Continuing in his support of the Trevor Project, in 2011 and 2012, Quinto gave emotional speeches at TrevorLIVE, a semiannual fund-raising event sponsored by the Trevor Project that brings together entertainers and corporate leaders in support of gay rights.

OBAMA PRIDE

During President Barack Obama's 2012 reelection campaign, Quinto joined other LGBTQ celebrities in backing the president, who had publically declared his support for same-sex marriage. The first time Quinto met Obama, the president—who happens to be a *Star Trek* fan—flashed Quinto the Vulcan salute! In a twelve-minute video spot called "Obama Pride," Quinto, along with Wanda Sykes, Jesse Tyler Ferguson, Billie Jean King, Chaz Bono,

Jane Lynch, and George Takei (who played Mr. Sulu on the original *Star Trek*), voices his support for Obama's reelection bid. The video celebrates the Obama administration's accomplishments in extending equal rights to LGBTQ citizens.

At the time of the election, Quinto also teamed up with openly gay and lesbian celebrities Ellen DeGeneres, Andy Cohen, Jane Lynch, and Neil Patrick Harris to produce a twelve-second video spoof of voter suppression, which aired on Jon Stewart's *Daily Show*. The spot, called "Voting Makes You Gay," was a comedic response to reports of scare tactics used by Republicans in North Carolina to prevent Democrats from going to the polls. The spoof features Cohen saying, "Because I voted, and now I'm gay," followed by Quinto declaring, "That's right, Republicans, voting makes you gay."

In the final days of the campaign, Quinto helped man the phones at the Obama campaign headquarters in Chicago. When Obama won the election, Quinto posted a picture of himself celebrating jubilantly in the confetti-filled convention center. He tweeted, "The great work begins," a famous line from *Angels in America*.

CHAPTER 8

ZACH'S MANY HATS

One might imagine that between filming two *Star Trek* movies, appearing regularly in the television series *American Horror Story*, and being a gay rights activist—not to mention shuttling regularly between Los Angeles and New York—Quinto would be a very busy man. But even before he scored the role of Spock, he decided to add another job title to his growing resume: producer. In 2008, Quinto formed a media production company with Corey Moosa and Neal Dodson, his good friends and fellow alumni from Carnegie Mellon drama school. They decided to name their company Before the Door (BTD), after the drama exercise they all knew from their freshman year at CMU. According to Quinto, he is the face of the company, Moosa is the heart, and Dodson is the brains.

Before he appeared in *Angels in America*, Quinto had a role in the first feature produced by BTD, *Margin Call* (2011). Written and directed by J. C. Chandor, the film features Kevin Spacey, Paul Bettany, Demi

Greeting avid fans at the premiere of *Margin Call* at the Berlin International Film Festival, Quinto demonstrates his left-handed autograph-signing technique.

Moore, and Jeremy Irons, among others. *Margin Call*'s background is the 2008 financial crisis that preceded the Great Recession in the United States. Quinto plays Peter Sullivan, a risk analyst in a fictional investment firm, watching it all come apart around him. The film's message was timely: it received rave reviews at the Sundance Film Festival, won two Independent Spirit Awards, and was nominated for an Academy Award for Best Original Screenplay.

J. C. Chandor also wrote and directed *All Is Lost*, another successful project from Before the Door. The 2013 film features Robert Redford as an unnamed sailor fighting for survival in the Indian Ocean after his sailboat is destroyed at sea. Redford's remarkable solo performance won the veteran actor a New York Film Critics

Circle Award as Best Actor. Many believe Redford deserved to be nominated for an Academy Award, but he was passed over. Other 2013 BTD projects include the found-footage marriage comedy *Breakup at a Wedding*, written and directed by Victor Quinaz, and Blair Erickson's horror film *Banshee Chapter*. Quinaz and Erickson are CMU alumni. Quinto estimates that at least 85 percent of BTD's projects have Carnegie Mellon connections.

Now BTD has multiple projects in the pipeline, including more films in development, television and web-based projects, and even a three-book graphic novel publishing deal. One TV project is a ten-part series called *The Chair* that will be filmed in Pittsburgh. The documentary series follows two young directors as each shoots a film about college students coming home to Pittsburgh for their first Thanksgiving break. Each director has the same script and the same budget of $850,000; audiences will get to see the whole moviemaking process and eventually vote on which film they like better.

QUINTO'S BROADWAY DEBUT

All along, Quinto made no secret of his desire to continue performing in live theater. Recently, he told the British paper the *Daily Mail*, "I've been doing theater since I was ten. Theater's my jam. It's my life, ultimately. If I could make a living just doing theater, I feel

IT GETS BETTER

In September 2010, syndicated columnist Dan Savage ("Savage Love") and his partner, Terry Miller, made a YouTube video to inspire hope in young people facing harassment for their sexual orientation. In the wake of several suicides of gay teens who had been bullied severely at school, Savage and Miller wanted to urge young people to hang on, and take heart, because "it gets better."

The It Gets Better Project became a worldwide movement, inspiring more than fifty thousand user-created videos that have been viewed more than fifty million times. Anyone can submit a video to the project (http://www.itgetsbetter.org), and many have, including President Barack Obama; Hillary Clinton; Adam Lambert; Ellen DeGeneres; the staffs of the Gap, Google, and Facebook; and Zachary Quinto.

like I really might." Quinto was cast as Tom Wingfield in the American Repertory Theater's revival of Tennessee Williams's play *The Glass Menagerie*, directed by Tony-winner John Tiffany. Tom Wingfield, who narrates the play, is an aspiring writer who works in a warehouse and dreams of escaping his overbearing mother and his fragile sister, Laura. The action takes place in St. Louis in 1937 and is drawn from Wingfield's memories. The production featured another Carnegie Mellon drama school graduate and veteran of *24*, Cherry Jones, in the role of Amanda Wingfield. Celia Keenan-Bolger played the painfully shy Laura, and Brian J. Smith was cast as the Gentleman Caller.

The play's title refers to the treasured collection of glass animals that are Laura's most prized possessions,

Applause and flowers are given to the cast of *The Glass Menagerie,* (*from left to right*) Celia Keenan-Bolger, Cherry Jones, Quinto, and Brian J. Smith, as they take their final bows on opening night at Broadway's Booth Theater.

a symbol of the fragile quality of human illusions. *The Glass Menagerie* previewed in Cambridge, Massachusetts, and eventually opened at the Booth Theater on Broadway on September 26, 2013, and soon garnered high praise from the critics for all four members of the cast. Ben Brantley of the *New York Times* wrote: "Mr. Quinto, best known for his screen work, is the finest Tom I've ever seen, a defensive romantic, sardonically in love with his own lush powers of description." The *Wall Street Journal* called Quinto's performance "revelatory." Performances were consistently sold out until the show closed its run on February 23, 2014.

Tennessee Williams was an American playwright who also wrote

A Streetcar Named Desire, Cat on a Hot Tin Roof, and many other plays that have been repeatedly produced onstage and made into films. *The Glass Menagerie,* which he termed a "memory play" and was based on his own family background, made him famous. Tom Wingfield is considered Williams's most autobiographical character. Williams, whose given name was Thomas (Tom), grew up in St. Louis. His neurotic and overbearing mother was a former Southern belle, like Amanda Wingfield, and he had a sister who suffered from schizophrenia. Williams was gay, and he struggled with prescription drug and alcohol dependency. Tom Wingfield tries to escape reality by drinking, and when he claims to be "at the movies" at two in the morning, it's clear that he's been with other men. To prepare for the role, Quinto spent time learning about the playwright's life, which helped enrich his portrayal of Tom.

QUINTO ON THE A-LIST

Zachary Quinto achieved his goal of returning to the New York stage. So what's in store for this multi-talented actor? He's heading back to Hollywood for a while. In addition to returning as Spock in the third *Star Trek* movie, Quinto appears opposite Rupert Friend in *Agent 47,* a sequel to the 2007 action movie *Hitman.*

10 THINGS YOU DON'T ALREADY KNOW ABOUT ZACHARY QUINTO

1. He is left-handed.
2. His favorite word is "brouhaha".
3. In honor of his Irish heritage, Quinto has a tattoo on his upper left arm of a Celtic triskele symbol.
4. If he wasn't an actor, he would probably be a psychiatrist.
5. Mother Teresa is his real-life hero: "God called her on her path. Once she listened to God and followed her life's purpose, she never heard from Him again. It was her faith in Him that kept her focused and committed."
6. He is learning to play the banjo.
7. His favorite film is *Harold and Maude*, the 1971 romantic comedy about a love affair between a death-obsessed younger man and an elderly woman.
8. If he could choose his superpower, it would be invisibility.
9. After appearing in *Angels in America*, Quinto spent a month alone in Peru and hiked the Inca Trail: "There were negative aspects of my life that I left behind me in the jungle."
10. Quinto would like his last words to be "N'at," a characteristic Pittsburgh expression meaning "and that." He has a bumper sticker on his car featuring that expression.

His production work with Before the Door will continue to keep Quinto busy. Eventually, he also wants to add "director" to his professional résumé: "I definitely want to direct, and I'm looking for ways to do that even now," he says. "For me, that's all about the story, and I haven't found the story yet...But I do want to explore that territory, and to find out, when the time is right, how to make that step."

One thing is certain: Zachary Quinto will continue to lend his voice to the chorus demanding equal rights for every member of the LGBTQ community. Despite recent strides made by the gay rights movement, much work remains to be done. The 2014 Winter Olympic Games held in Sochi, Russia, became the focus of international protests when Russian president Vladimir Putin signed into law a bill prohibiting pro-gay "propaganda" and restricting gay rights activity. Soon after, Putin signed legislation preventing Russian children from being adopted by gay couples or by anyone who lives in a country where marriage equality exists in any form. These laws mean that in Russia if you

Quinto's personal experiences with antigay discrimination have helped make him a passionate spokesperson for the cause of LGBTQ rights.

are gay, you can be fined, imprisoned, or have your children taken away from you. Quinto joined other prominent actors, celebrities, and politicians in protesting this homophobic legislation.

Quinto believes that his own decision to come out has enriched both his personal and his professional life, and everyone deserves the same freedom to embrace his or her true identity without fear of persecution or discrimination. That's definitely something worth fighting for.

TIMELINE

1977 Zachary John Quinto is born on June 2 in Pittsburgh, Pennsylvania.

1984 Zachary's father, Joe Quinto Sr., dies of kidney cancer when Zachary is seven years old.

1988 As a member of the Pittsburgh Civic Light Opera Mini Stars, Quinto makes his stage debut as a Munchkin in *The Wizard of Oz*. It is the first of many plays and musicals in which he will appear.

1994 Quinto wins the Gene Kelly Award for Best Supporting Actor in *The Pirates of Penzance*. After surviving a serious car accident, he decides to become a professional actor.

1995 Quinto graduates from Central Catholic High School in Pittsburgh.

He enrolls as a freshman at Carnegie Mellon University School of Drama.

1996 Quinto befriends fellow CMU drama students Corey Moosa and Neal Dodson.

1999 Quinto performs in his drama school Senior Showcases in Los Angeles and New York. He receives more positive responses to his Los Angeles Showcase. Quinto graduates from the drama program at CMU with a bachelor of fine arts (BFA) degree in musical theater.

2000 Quinto moves to L.A. to pursue an acting career.

2003 After a series of bit parts and disappointments, he scores his first recurring television role in the part of Adam Kaufman on the action series *24* starring Kiefer Sutherland.

2006 Quinto appears in the faux-reality show *So NoTORIous*, with Tori Spelling. Just before his thirtieth birthday, he is cast as the villain Sylar on *Heroes*.

2007   Quinto wins a Future Classic Award for *Heroes*. He is named one of *People* magazine's "Sexiest Men Alive."After actively campaigning for the role, Quinto wins the part of Mr. Spock in J. J. Abrams's *Star Trek* film. On July 26 at a comic convention, he first meets the original Spock, Leonard Nimoy.

2007–2008   The Writers Guild of America strike lasts three months, from November 5, 2007, to February 12, 2008. During the hiatus, while *Heroes* is on hold, *Star Trek: The Future Begins* is filmed. Quinto appears on the cover of consecutive issues of *Entertainment Weekly*, first as Sylar and then as Spock.

Quinto, Neal Dodson, and Corey Moosa form the Before the Door production company.

2009   *Star Trek: The Future Begins* is released on May 8.

2010   On October 28, *Angels in America* opens, with Quinto playing the part of Louis Ironson.

2011   Quinto appears as Peter Sullivan in *Margin Call*, the first film released by Before the Door. He joins the cast of *American Horror Story* and plays Chad Warwick in season one. During an interview with *New York* magazine, Quinto comes out as a gay man.

2013   On May 16, the second *Star Trek* film, *Star Trek into Darkness*, is released. Quinto returns to *American Horror Story* to play Dr. Oliver Thredson in season two. He also makes his Broadway debut on September 26, 2013, as Tom Wingfield in *The Glass Menagerie*.

antagonist An enemy or a rival; the person who opposes the hero or protagonist of a drama.

closeted Being or functioning in private or in secret. A closeted gay person has not publically disclosed his or her sexual orientation.

coming out "Coming out of the closet," or simply "coming out," is a figure of speech for disclosing one's sexual orientation and/or gender identity.

cyberbullying Electronically posting—using cell phones, computers, or tablets—mean-spirited messages about a person that are meant to threaten or intimidate. Cyberbullies often remain anonymous.

Don't Ask, Don't Tell (DADT) Name for the former official U.S. policy (1993–2011) regarding the service of homosexuals in the military. The policy prohibited military personnel from discriminating against closeted homosexuals serving in the armed forces; it also barred any homosexual or bisexual person from disclosing his or her sexual orientation while serving in the military. A congressional bill to repeal DADT was enacted in 2010, and the policy was terminated on September 20, 2011.

gaybashing Verbal or physical abuse against a person who is perceived by the aggressor as gay, lesbian, or bisexual.

hate crime A criminal offense against a person or property motivated by an offender's bias against race, religion, sexual orientation, ethnic origin, or other prejudice.

headshot A photograph of someone's face, typically a promotional photograph of a model, actor, or author.

homophobia Hatred or fear of homosexuals, sometimes leading to acts of violence and expressions of hostility.

LGBTQ An acronym that stands for "lesbian, gay, bisexual, transgender, queer and/or questioning." It originated in the 1990s as a more inclusive replacement for the term "the gay community."

marriage equality Legal recognition of the right of two people of the same sex to marry.

off-Broadway A professional venue in New York City with a seating capacity between 100 and 499. Off-Broadway theaters are smaller than Broadway theaters. Even smaller venues are known as Off-Off-Broadway theaters.

pre-production The work done on a film or a broadcast program before full-scale production begins.

production company A company involved in producing live or recorded entertainment. Production companies for films and television typically provide the money for a project and make decisions about which director and actors can be hired.

queer A term once used to degrade and deride homosexuals, "queer" has been adopted as an umbrella term that avoids more fixed labels, such

as "gay," "lesbian," and "bisexual." "Queer" is a
more fluid category, meaning someone who identi-
fies herself or himself as outside the societal
norms of gender, sexuality, and/or even politics.

showcase An annual event that displays the skills
and talents of aspiring actors to an audience of
industry professionals.

Sundance Film Festival An annual film festival
held in Park City, Utah. Sundance is one of the
largest independent film festivals in the United
States. It showcases new work from American and
international independent filmmakers.

Trekkie An avid fan of the science fiction television
program *Star Trek* or one of its spin-off series
or films.

TV pilot A stand-alone episode of a television series
used to sell the show to a TV network; also known
as just a pilot.

Vulcan salute An iconic gesture originated by
Mr. Spock in the original *Star Trek* TV series. It
consists of a raised hand, palm forward, with the
fingers parted between the middle and ring fingers
and the thumb extended. Often accompanied with
the words, "Live long and prosper."

Carnegie Mellon University School of Drama
Purnell Center for the Arts
Carnegie Mellon University
5000 Forbes Avenue
Pittsburgh, PA 15213
(412) 268-2068
Website: http://www.drama.cmu.edu
Founded in 1914, the Carnegie Mellon University
School of Drama is the oldest conservatory training, and the first degree-granting drama
institution, in the United States. The school
combines established practice with innovation
and pedagogical and technological advancement
across all disciplines.

Egale Canada
Canada Human Rights Trust
185 Carlton Street
Toronto, ON M5A 2K7
Canada
(416) 964-7887
(888) 204-7777
Website: http://egale.ca
This Canadian lesbian, gay, bisexual, and transgender (LGBT) human rights organization was
founded in 1986. Egale Canada was the driving
force behind the Canadians for Equal Marriage
campaign, which resulted in Canada becoming

one of the first nations in the world to legalize same-sex marriage.

Gay-Straight Alliance Network
1550 Bryant Street, Suite 600
San Francisco, CA 94103
(415) 552-4229
Website: http://www.gsanetwork.org
The Gay-Straight Alliance Network provides information on how to start a Gay-Straight Alliance at a school, how to work with other Gay-Straight Alliances locally, and how to fight discrimination and abuse in schools.

It Gets Better Project
110 S. Fairfax Avenue, Suite A11-71
Los Angeles, CA 90036
Website: http://www.itgetsbetter.org
The mission of the It Gets Better Project is to communicate to lesbian, gay, bisexual, and transgender youth around the world that it gets better, and to create and inspire the changes needed to make it better for them.

Matthew Shephard Foundation
1530 Blake Street, Suite 200
Denver, CO 80202
(303) 830-7400

Website: http://www.matthewshephard.org

The organization was founded by Judy and Dennis Shephard, in memory of their son Matthew, who was murdered in an antigay hate crime in October 1998. The foundation seeks to "replace hate with understanding, compassion, and acceptance" through its varied educational, outreach, and advocacy programs and by continuing to tell Matthew's story. The site also provides resources for those wishing to produce the play *The Laramie Project or The Laramie Project: Ten Years Later.*

National Gay and Lesbian Task Force

1325 Massachusetts Avenue NW, Suite 600

Washington, DC 20005

(202) 393-5177

Website: http://www.thetaskforce.org

With several chapters across the United States, the National Gay and Lesbian Task Force supports the GLBT community by training activists, organizing campaigns to promote pro-gay legislation, and providing research and policy analysis.

PFLAG (Parents, Families, and Friends of Lesbians and Gays)

PFLAG National Office

1828 L Street NW, Suite 660

Washington, DC 20036

(202) 467-8180

Website: http://community.pflag.org

Founded in 1972 by a mother publically supporting her gay son, PFLAG is the nation's largest
family and ally organization. Today this vast
grassroots network has more than 350 chapters
and 200,000 members and supporters in all
fifty states.

PFLAG Canada

440 Albert Street, Suite 304C

Ottawa, ON K1R 5B5

(888) 530-6777

Website: http://www.pflagcanada.org

This national charitable organization was founded by
parents who wanted to help themselves and their
family members understand and accept their
non-heterosexual children. PFLAG supports,
educates, and provides resources for individuals
with questions and concerns.

The Trevor Project

P.O. Box 69232

West Hollywood, CA 90069

(310) 271-8845

(866) 488-7386

Website: http://www.thetrevorproject.org

Founded in 1998 by the creators of the Academy
Award–winning short film *Trevor*, the Trevor
Project is the leading national organization providing crisis intervention and suicide prevention
services to LGBTQ young people ages thirteen to
twenty-four.

WEBSITES

Because of the changing nature of Internet links, Rosen
Publishing has developed an online list of websites
related to the subject of this book. This site is updated
regularly. Please use this link to access the list:

http://www.rosenlinks.com/LGBT/Quin

OR FURTHER READING

Alsenas, Linas. *Gay America: Struggle for Equality.* New York, NY: Amulet Books, 2008.

Belge, Kathy, and Marke Bieschke. *Queer: The Ultimate LGBT Guide for Teens.* San Francisco, CA: Zest Books, 2011.

Bornstein, Kate. *Hello, Cruel World: 101 Alternatives to Suicide for Teens, Freaks and Other Outlaws.* New York, NY: Seven Stories Press, 2006.

Brown, D. W. *You Can Act!: A Complete Guide for Actors.* Studio City, CA: Michael Wiese Productions, 2009.

Calin, Marisa. *Between You & Me.* New York, NY: Bloomsbury USA, 2012.

Halpin, Mikki. *It's Your World—If You Don't Like It, Change It: Activism for Teenagers.* New York, NY: Simon & Schuster, 2008.

Huegel, Kelly. *GLBTQ: The Survival Guide for Gay, Lesbian, Bisexual, Transgender, and Questioning Teens.* Minneapolis, MN: Free Spirit Publishing, 2011.

Lynch, Radclyffe, and Katherine E. Lynch, eds. *OMG Queer: Stories for Queer Youth by Queer Youth.* Valley Falls, NY: Bold Strokes, 2012.

Marcus, Eric. *What If Someone I Know Is Gay? Answers to Questions About What It Means to Be Gay and Lesbian.* New York, NY: Simon Pulse, 2007.

Moon, Sarah, ed. *The Letter Q: Queer Writers' Notes to Their Younger Selves.* New York, NY: Scholastic, 2012.

Planned Parenthood of Toronto. *Hear Me Out: True Stories of Teens Educating and Confronting Homophobia.* Toronto, ON, Canada: Second Story Press, 2003.

Powell, Michael. *The Acting Bible: The Complete Resource for Aspiring Actors.* Hauppauge, NY: Barron's Educational Series, 2010.

Savage, Dan, and Terry Miller, eds. *It Gets Better: Coming Out, Overcoming Bullying, and Creating a Life Worth Living.* New York, NY: Dutton Adult, 2011.

Schwartz, John. *Oddly Normal: One Family's Struggle to Help Their Teenage Son Come to Terms with His Sexuality.* New York, NY: Penguin, 2012.

Telgemeier, Raina. *Drama.* New York, NY: Scholastic Graphix, 2012.

Billard, Mary. "Zachary Quinto: A Playwright's Home, an Actor's Muse." *New York Times*, September 18, 2013. Retrieved January 29, 2014 (http://www.nytimes.com).

Brevet, Brad. "EXCL: Sylar Speaks! Zachary Quinto Talks 'Heroes' and Spock." *Rope of Silicon*, August 22, 2007. Retrieved January 22, 2014 (http://www.ropeofsilicon.com).

Carpenter, Mackenzie. "Actor Quinto, Local Groups Back 'The Chair' Film Project. *Pittsburgh Post-Gazette*, January 13, 2014. Retrieved February 6, 2014 (http://www.post-gazette.com).

Daily Mail Reporter. "'Star Trek' Was a Means to an End to Me." *Daily Mail*, September 26, 2013. Retrieved January 31, 2014 (http://www.dailymail.co.uk).

Day, Elizabeth. "Zachary Quinto: Boldly Going Where Other Actors Fear To." *Guardian*, May 4, 2013. Retrieved January 29, 2014 (http://www.theguardian.com/culture).

Douglas, Edward. "An Exclusive Interview with Zachary Quinto, Producer." Comingsoon.net, June 20, 2013. Retrieved January 22, 2014 (http://www.comingsoon.net).

Hicklin, Aaron. "Zachary Quinto: Star Man." *Out*, September 12, 2012. Retrieved January 25, 2014 (http://www.out.com).

Huver, Scott. "Spock on Spock: Leonard Nimoy and Zachary Quinto Sound Off." *People*, May 8, 2009. Retrieved February 2, 2014 (http://www.people.com).

Keegan, Rebecca. "Zachary Quinto Rides a Wave of Professional, Personal Growth." *Los Angeles Times*, October 20, 2011. Retrieved January 20, 2014 (http://articles.latimes.com).

Kit, Zorianna. "A Minute with: Zachary Quinto on 'Star Trek,' Spock and Coming Out." Reuters, May 15, 2013. Retrieved January 20, 2014 (http://www.reuters.com).

Lachonis, Jon. "Exclusive Interview! 'Heroes' Sylar–Zachary Quinto." *Buddy TV*, April 23, 2007. Retrieved January 29, 2014 (http://www.buddytv.com).

Letizia, Anthony. "Zachary Quinto, Pittsburgh, and Star Trek." *Geek Pittsburgh*, May 15, 2013. Retrieved February 3, 2014 (http://www.geekpittsburgh.com).

NPR Staff. "Quinto Turns Inward to Find Spock's Soul." *All Things Considered*, May 17, 2013. Retrieved January 15, 2014 (http://www.npr.org).

Riley, Jenelle. "Zachary Quinto Talks 'Star Trek,' Coming Out, and the Return of 'Heroes.'" *Backstage*, May 16, 2013. Retrieved January 25, 2014 (http://www.backstage.com).

Rooney, David. "Career Zigzag, Changing Coasts and Galaxies." *New York Times*, October 21, 2010. Retrieved February 1, 2014 (http://www.nytimes.com).

Siddiqui, Sabrina. "Zachary Quinto, 'Star Trek into Darkness' Star: Gay Marriage Is an Unstoppable Wave." *Huffington Post*, May 16, 2013. Retrieved February 1, 2014 (http://www .huffingtonpost.com).

Streitfeld, David. "For Pittsburgh, There's Life After Steel." *New York Times*, January 7, 2009. Retrieved January 19, 2014 (http://www .nytimes.com).

Travers, Peter. Interview with Zachary Quinto. *Popcorn with Peter Travers* (video), May 20, 2013. Retrieved January 15, 2014. (http://zach-quinto.com).

TrekMovie.com staff. "Nimoy on Working with Quinto." *TrekMovie.com*, September 15, 2008. Retrieved January 20, 2014 (http://trekmovie.com).

Wallace, Benjamin. "What's Up, Spock?" *New York Magazine*, October 19, 2011. Retrieved January 20, 2014 (http://www.nymag.com).

INDEX

ABOUT THE AUTHOR

Monique Vescia is a writer with many nonfiction books, on a variety of subjects, to her credit. Like Zachary Quinto, she was born in Pennsylvania, the child of an Irish mother and an Italian father. She now makes her home in Seattle, Washington, with her husband and their teenage son.

PHOTO CREDITS

Cover Robin Marchant/Getty Images; p. 7 Charley Gallay/Getty Images; pp. 11, 22–23, 32–33, 52, 61, 72–73 © AP Images; p. 14 Jim Spellman/WireImage/Getty Images; pp. 16–17 Rex Features/AP Images; p. 19 © Everett Collection; p. 20 Donaldson Collection/Michael Ochs Archives/Getty Images; p. 27 photo by Louis Stein; pp. 30–31, 69 Astrid Stawiarz/Getty Images; p. 37 Larry Busacca/Getty Images; p. 39 BuzzFoto/FilmMagic/Getty Images; p. 41 Michael Buckner/Getty Images; p. 45 Alberto E. Rodriguez/Getty Images; p. 47 © AF Archive/Alamy; p. 50 Bunny, PacificCoast News/Newscom; pp. 56–57 CBS Photo Archive/Getty Images; pp. 58–59 M. Phillips/WireImage/Getty Images; pp. 64–65 Amanda Edwards/Getty Images; pp. 78–79 Mark Davis/Getty Images; pp. 82–83 © Andreas Teich/Action Press/ZUMA Press; pp. 86–87 Ben Gabbe/Getty Images; pp. 90–91 Frazer Harrison/Getty Images; cover and interior graphic elements © iStockphoto.com/traffic_analyzer (colored stripes), © iStockphoto.com/rusm (pebbled texture).

Designer: Nicole Russo; Editor: Nicholas Croce; Photo Researcher: Amy Feinberg